ME TOO
BUT **NEVER** AGAIN

Intimate Stories From Women Who Have Overcome Abuse and Sexual Trauma

Hanna Olivas & Adriana Luna Carlos
Along with 8 Other Inspiring Women Warriors

© 2022 ALL RIGHTS RESERVED.

Published by She Rises Studios Publishing www.SheRisesStudios.com.

No part of this book may be reproduced or transmitted in any form whatsoever, electronic, or mechanical, including photocopying, recording, or by any informational storage or retrieval system without the expressed written, dated and signed permission from the publisher and co-authors.

LIMITS OF LIABILITY/DISCLAIMER OF WARRANTY:

The co-authors and publisher of this book have used their best efforts in preparing this material. While every attempt has been made to verify the information provided in this book, neither the co-authors nor the publisher assumes any responsibility for any errors, omissions, or inaccuracies.

The co-authors and publisher make no representation or warranties with respect to the accuracy, applicability, or completeness of the contents of this book. They disclaim any warranties (expressed or implied), merchantability, or for any purpose. The co-authors and publisher shall in no event be held liable for any loss or other damages, including but not limited to special, incidental, consequential, or other damages.

ISBN: 979-8-9869367-4-1

Table of Contents

INTRODUCTION 5

PSYCHOLOGICAL WARFARE 9
   By Adriana Luna Carlos 9

SHATTERED NOT BROKEN 14
   By Hanna Olivas 14

WHEN I LEARNED TO PRAY 21
   By Rebecca Chandler 21

BIRD SET FREE 28
   By Jaime Lynne 28

I AM SEEN, I AM HEARD 36
   By Isabelle Ruiz 36

HELPING WOMEN HEAL FROM CHILD SEXUAL ABUSE .. 45
   By Nicole Curtis 45

DEFY IMPOSSIBLE CIRCUMSTANCES 50
   By Madison Clark 50

MOVING THROUGH MY FEARS FREED ME TO
FIND MY SELF 56
   By Divya Chandegra 56

FINDING PURPOSE FROM THE PAIN OF THE PAST 64
   By Rachel Farnsworth 64

HIDING PAIN DOES DAMAGE 70
   By Frances Helena 70

JOIN THE MOVEMENT! #BAUW 78

INTRODUCTION

She Rises Studios was created and inspired by the mother-daughter duo Hanna Olivas and Adriana Luna Carlos. In the middle of 2020, when the world was at one of its most vulnerable times, we saw the need to embrace women globally by offering inspirational quotes, blogs, and articles. Then, in March of 2021, we launched our very own Women's Empowerment Podcast: *She Rises Studios Podcast*.

It is now one of the most sought out Women based podcasts both nationally and internationally. You can find us on your favorite podcast platforms, such as Spotify, Google Podcasts, Apple Podcasts, IHeartRadio, and much more! We didn't stop there. Establishing a safe space for women has become an even deeper need. Due to a global pandemic, women lost their businesses, employment, homes, finances, spouses, and more.

We decided to form the She Rises Studios Community Facebook Group. An environment strictly for women about women. Our focus in this group is to educate and celebrate women globally. To meet them exactly where they are on their journey.

It's a group of Ordinary Women Doing EXTRAordinary Things.

As we continued to grow our network, we saw a need to help shape the minds and influences of women struggling with insecurities, doubts, fears, etc. From this, we created a global movement known as:

Me Too But Never Again

Being a Warrior means you have battled a war most have not. It can be a physical, mental, emotional, or spiritual war.

How we choose to fight our battle makes all the difference in the turnout. These types of war are most often unexpected and very treacherous.

We can feel pain, fear, shame, unworthy, overwhelmed, and alone while going through the battlefield.

Me Too But Never Again is a book for those who have experienced the war of sexual abuse, assault, rape, molestation, human trafficking, and or violent crimes.

We asked women from all over the world to share their journey of healing, overcoming, and living a life after the pain. These women have learned how to forgive, love, and live a full life.

They have gone through tragedy to triumph and want to help others do the same.

This book's power is truth, bravery, love, faith, and learning to forgive so women can move forward and live a life of purpose, laughter, peace, and joy.

We, as women, are meant to experience a thriving and powerful life. We did not choose to be victims, but we can choose to be Warriors.

The courage to fight a battle that is unseen to many is, Me Too But Never Again.

She Rises Studios offers:
- She Rises Studios Publishing
- She Rises Studios Public Relations
- She Rises Studios Podcast
- She Rises Studios Magazine
- Becoming An Unstoppable Woman TV Show
- She Rises Studios Community
- She Rises Studios Academy

We won't stop encouraging women to be Unstoppable. This is just the beginning of our global movement.

She Rises, She Leads, She Lives...

With Love,
HANNA OLIVAS
ADRIANA LUNA CARLOS
SHE RISES STUDIOS
www.sherisesstudios.com

Adriana Luna Carlos

Founder and CEO of She Rises Studios

https://www.linkedin.com/company/she-rises-studios/
https://www.instagram.com/sherisesstudios/
https://www.facebook.com/sherisesstudios
www.SheRisesStudios.com

Adriana Luna Carlos is a much sought-after expert in Web and Graphic design as well as a new Podcast Host Personnel for She Rises Studios. For over 10 years she has embraced her passion in the digital arts field along with helping women worldwide overcome their insecure idiosyncrasies. Today, when she's not spending time with her family and friends, you'll often find her helping woman focus on rising up and becoming unafraid of success. To learn more about Adriana Luna Carlos and how she can help you overcome obstacles in your business, mindset, or insecurities, visit www.SheRisesStudios.com

PSYCHOLOGICAL WARFARE

By Adriana Luna Carlos

As a child, you stole my sanity; as a teen, you exploited my puberty; as an adult, you left me with psychological scars,
I will suffer no longer.

Throughout the years, you've haunted my dreams, kept me up in fear, and drifted my family apart,
I will fight you no more.

Many days and nights it has taken me to see past your wrongdoings, to find love and happiness, and though it may seem like forgiveness,
I will grant you no access.

I used to be afraid to make eye contact for too long. I felt that the eyes could tell all, and I knew I was keeping a lot inside. I remember so many times, more than I can count on two hands, that my dad would say to me, "if anyone ever touches you or does something bad to you, tell me, even if they are family." The problem with this was that the abuse had already begun.

"You are the prettiest girl in Pasadena." Without context, this sentence sounds normal and maybe even flattering. But for me, this sentence was repulsive. My perpetrator would say this to me just as he would start to harass me sexually. Psychological warfare was the game he played with a 5-year-old up until the age of 15.

I wasn't safe anywhere that I went. Whether I was sitting on the couch watching TV with my brother, or washing dishes, he would come up behind me and whisper in my ear or rub his body against mine. I would shout, "leave me alone!" If someone turned to see what he was doing, he would laugh it off and make people think he was being silly and playful. They were none the wiser. I tried so many times in my own way to alert my family of his actions, but nothing seemed to register with them.

I often told myself that I would rather he did this to me than to someone else in my family. I knew that he was not doing this because it was me specifically; he was doing this because he was sick in the head. Occasionally, I would straight out ask him why he was doing this, and I told him, "You know this is wrong, right? Family members are NOT supposed to do things like this." He would just smile and laugh it off and say, "no, it's ok, we are not doing anything wrong."

I recall a day in high school when we spoke on the topic of molestation with classmates and one of our teachers. It wasn't a regular class, it must have been some sort of outreach program to help kids like myself, I just hadn't known that yet. I remember the teacher talking about how 1 in 3 people are victims of sexual abuse and she said, "that means that one-third of you in this room right now may have been victims of sexual abuse."

At that moment, I felt frozen. I had never spoken to anyone about this, let alone was I ready for an open discussion on the topic. I listened intently as the girls in the room started to open up about family members and friends and some even told stories about themselves. It was sad and also empowering all at the same time. I wanted so badly to speak up and share my story so that others wouldn't feel scared or alone. But I couldn't, I wasn't prepared yet.

After this day, there was a shift in my mind. I had found a new type of anger and a new fight within myself. Whenever he would try to abuse me, I would shut it down faster, louder, and more confidently. I told him to "leave me alone or I am telling my dad!" He would tell me, "you little bitch, no, you won't." Any time I would deny him or tell him off, he would call me by that name.

So smug he thought I would never have the courage to speak up for myself.

May 11, 2009, was the day my life would change forever. My aunt had called me to ask me a random question but she somehow could tell that I wanted to say something. She kept telling me to spit it out, but I wouldn't. She said, "ok, well, I am on my way to pick you up, be ready in 10 minutes." I was inside the house, running to the front porch, and as I was about to take my step to the stairs, he says to me, "you're not going to stay at your aunt's house and talk to no boys." I remember thinking to myself, "I will NEVER have to hear your voice again or see your face." I ran so fast down the stairs and shouted, "BYE!"

I had a letter in my hand that was meant for my dad to read. I had held onto that letter for two weeks before having handed it off to my aunt. In that handwritten letter were lots of memories that I was going to share with my dad, of what his dad did to me, my grandfather.

I wrote about how I was afraid to say anything at all because I thought he would attack my grandfather and end up in jail.

Once my aunt read this letter, she immediately started crying and got on the phone. She asked my grandfather, "how could you do this to her??" and a bunch of other comments that truly break my heart. She told me that I wouldn't be going home until things get resolved and then she called my dad. My heart sank, I felt petrified, ashamed, and afraid he wouldn't believe me and so many more things ran through my head.

When my dad showed up, I walked up to him and went into his arms, and started balling. He knew something bad had happened but he hadn't realized it was to me or what it was even about. I had to break the news and tell him what his dad and done to me. Just thinking about this moment makes all the emotions rise up again. There was so much heartbreak this night.

My grandfather took many years from me, lots of childhood moments, innocence, safety and so much more. He stole from me and my family. Though it seemed like I would never be able to heal from this, each day I would pray to my grandma and ask her to help me and guide me. She passed away when I was only four years old but I remember her so well. She was my protector and my safety. Without her love, I fear I would have been a different person and may have never been able to cope the way that I have.

Having felt the lows of sorrow and the highs of tomorrow,
I safely admit my heart is heavy and pulses for the pursuit of happiness.

I track the moves of my yesterdays and plan the intentions of my next days.
Peacefully, I thank you for the truths you have availed to me.

Gracefully, I take temporary defeat, as I know and am able to see,
Our future is not yet written in stone, I don't concede.

This life is meant for more than mediocracy, this I truly believe.

Hanna Olivas

Founder and CEO of She Rises Studios

https://www.linkedin.com/company/she-rises-studios/
https://www.instagram.com/sherisesstudios
https://www.facebook.com/sherisesstudios
www.SheRisesStudios.com

Author, Speaker, and Founder. Hanna was born and raised in Las Vegas, Nevada, and has paved her way to becoming one of the most influential women of 2023. Hanna is the co-founder of She Rises Studios and the founder of the Brave & Beautiful Blood Cancer Foundation. Her journey started in 2017 when she was first diagnosed with Multiple Myeloma, an incurable blood cancer. Now more than ever, her focus is to empower other women to become leaders because The Future is Female. She is currently traveling and speaking publicly to women to educate them on entrepreneurship, leadership, and owning the female power within.

SHATTERED NOT BROKEN

By Hanna Olivas

"Stop, I can't breathe. You are hurting me." These words I spoke at the young age of four. I begged many times, saying these exact words to a man who stole my innocence repeatedly.

"Mommy, it hurts down there." "Mommy, help me." "Please, Mommy, I'm sorry."

As I write this chapter, I am reminded of every ounce of pain I endured and had to relive again until I was eight. Every bath he gave me, every time he held me down, every time he used his hand or objects, I prayed to God to take me away. Every time he touched me, he took a piece of me away. I was his target, his focus, and his obsession. I felt dirty, scared, violated, and alone. I had no idea what to do or how to stop it. I only knew it felt wrong, and it hurt.

The abuse finally stopped, but the pain physically, mentally, and emotionally continued. In fact, at times, I can still smell his stench and feel his touch as if it was happening now. I often have to remind myself that it's no longer happening. I am safe and loved; I am on a healing journey.

Through the years, I felt marked as if the whole world knew I was this dirty little girl.

Physically he caused long-term problems from the sexual abuse. I had to heal from second and third-degree vaginal tearing. I was anxious and depressed and suffered from years of night terrors and panic attacks.

I was afraid to be alone, afraid of bath time, fearful of the dark, scared of men. I operated in total fear. I carried this into my young teenage years straight into an adult woman. I was a guarded, dirty, damaged girl. I was so angry at my mom, dad, and grandparents for not protecting me. In fact, I grew a pure hatred for them and the man who violated me.

As the years went by, I became rebellious, promiscuous, hateful, and careless. I didn't care if I lived or died. I just wanted the pain and memories to stop. But they just wouldn't. I became a runway and was eventually taken by the juvenile court system and held for long periods of time.

I questioned God, faith, and people in general. I had no trust in myself. I wasn't given the option for help or therapy until I was 14, and by then, I didn't want it or understand how it could help me. I was permanently marked and damaged goods.

I always wondered, why me? Why anyone? Why does this type of evil exist in the world?

Unfortunately, I wasn't a Me Too victim once I was raped at the age of fourteen by someone I knew and again by a man whom I married at a very young age. It hurts my heart deeply to even write this because it's so unbelievably hard to fathom. All the abuse and rape I suffered finally stopped at the age of 21 years old. You can imagine how messed up I was. Two of my beautiful children are a product of years of forced rape.

Now a young mother who had no idea of how to even take care of myself, let alone two children.

By this time, I was always operating in fight or flight mode, and I finally reached out to the one person I thought would help me, my mother. I called and asked her, "can I please come home?" Her reply was cold and so detached. She said "no" and hung up the phone.

It was then, and there I realized I would never again be a victim!!! But

I was wrong. I had no idea how to start, but I knew I needed to get the hell out of the marriage and away from his darkness.

What a struggle it was to break the chains I was bonded by.

For the first time since a little girl, I prayed for God to give me the courage to fight back and leave for good. I escaped with my two young children and nothing else. I had to start over from scratch. I was so terrified on so many levels. But I knew if I didn't leave, I would always stay a victim.

Little did I know that was just the beginning of more heartache. I thought by escaping my last perpetrator I'd be free. But I wasn't, and in fact, he made my life so difficult. I became even more depressed, and a downward spiral effect happened. I had lost custody of my children and my mind, body, and soul.

I was so angry at the time I'd lost my children and even more angry at how they'd suffered at the hands of a man who forced himself on me over and over. I remember how sick I was from the stress. I ended up in the hospital so often for panic attacks, unexplained illnesses, rashes, hair loss, and more. I spent years fighting and trying to heal and live and see my children. It wasn't until years and thousands of mistakes later that I would see my children and finally be their mother.

All those years as a victim and barely surviving. Most days, I felt numb and ashamed. I was shattered. The fragile glass had finally been shattered. I remember one day asking myself, will it get better than this? Will I survive all these years of mental, physical, and sexual abuse?

How do I fix my shattered life? Does anyone out there love me? Am I safe?

The answer is yes, but it wasn't going to be easy. I finally made a choice to seek help.

I remember going to my first therapy appointment. I kept saying to myself, "I won't share it all. They will think I'm crazy". The truth is, I wanted to share everything that happened to me, and in my first appointment, it all came out like vomit.

I spent years in therapy, church, and prayer. I also spent years running from myself. Making more bad choices in life and men. I just wanted to be loved and healed. When would it be my turn? I became a mother two more times in my journey.

It wasn't until the birth of my youngest son that it all changed. As I was leaving the hospital and I remember thinking I was shattered but not broken. It's time to pick up the pieces and start healing once and for all. I wanted to be a better mother, and I wanted to be able to breathe.

I went back to therapy and church. I joined women's Bible studies. I did everything I could to heal. I worked two, sometimes three, jobs to survive and care for my children as a single mom. Everything I earned by handwork. I bought a car, we lived in a tiny apartment, and we had food, water, and electricity. I did the very best I could with the means I had.

One day I was in church listening to the pastor speak on forgiveness. The kids were in youth group, and I was in service alone, listening to his message. How we must learn to forgive if we want to be forgiven. I thought to myself, "Fuck That" I want the men who hurt me to suffer. Oh, I was so angry. I thought, how can a pastor say this? Does he know what I've been through? Are you seriously saying I have to forgive the men whole stole my innocence, years of my life, and years of pain? When the service was over, I immediately grabbed my kids, and I left angry.

How can anyone forgive those things? Why do the perps get to be forgiven? Months went by before I stepped into the church and as soon as I did, a woman from Bible study asked if we were ok. She hadn't seen us for a while. I told her yes. She asked why we were absent, so I told her the truth. Again it all came out like vomit.

This woman began to cry, and she reached out to embrace me with the warmest, safest hug I'd received in years. For the first time ever, I felt safe. It was definitely a day I'll never forget. She then asked if she could pray with me, and I agreed. Hearing her prayer amazed me; it was like she knew my every hurt, thought, and fear.

From then forward, I went to church and women's groups, continued therapy, and really focused on how to forgive the unforgivable. Every day has been a work in progress. I lived the first thirty-seven years of my life in fear, anger, judgment, regret, unforgiveness, and more.

I believe and know what kept me fighting and trying was my children. Their love for me was greater than any pain I'd experienced. They showed me forgiveness, unconditional love, and just how beautiful life could be.

Once I realized how to ask for help and how to open up, I began to heal. I learned that I was shattered but never truly broken. Thank you to the woman at church for not seeing me as the marked dirty girl. But for seeing me as a woman and mother who wanted more for herself and her children.

Every step I've taken since that day has been to heal and forgive. I can truly tell you no one should bare this burden alone. If you have been the victim of sexual abuse, please, please speak up. Tell someone who can help you!! There is help out there, I promise you. Don't keep silent. Scream out for help. Whisper if it's unsafe but let someone know.

Since I began my healing journey and completed years of therapy, I now travel and speak to other women. I teach them to use their voice. How to speak up, how to leave, or even escape. To know they are not alone. I am here as your Me Too But Never Again Warrior. You are not alone. You are loved and worthy. To those reading this book who've Never experienced sexual abuse or trauma like this, please educate yourself and look around. Be the voice and advocate for those who can't.

I am asking the readers of this book to please unite with us. Help us be a voice, help us reach those who are being affected. Expose human trafficking, expose the perpetrators, expose the evil. Shield the victims. Fight for them. Don't ignore this. We need more counselors, shelters, safe homes, education, finances, and professionals to step in and help Me Too But Never Again Warriors.

I am no longer afraid, I am no longer a victim, and I have chosen forgiveness for me, not them. I have learned to forgive those who didn't protect me. Has it been easy? Absolutely not. Do I struggle and still feel the hurt and pain? Yes, I do. But I have chosen to live in forgiveness and healing. To stop blaming myself and to accept the things I couldn't control.

My hope in creating and writing this book is to expose this sexual epidemic for what it truly is. To stop human trafficking, to prevent rape and molestation if possible. To stop violent attacks on women and children. To hold severer punishments for perpetrators. To place laws and higher safety measures. To teach families how to communicate and educate their children.

How do you ask? By being a voice together, by getting involved. You can start in your own home and community by gaining knowledge yourself instead of turning a blind eye.

We can no longer look the other way, and we must stand up and fight together.

We are Me Too But Never Again Warriors

Rebecca Chandler

Owner of Wholistic Finance & Wholistic Arizona Healing Ranch

https://www.facebook.com/rebecca.chandler.585
https://www.linkedin.com/in/rebecca-chandler-80207b229/
https://wholisticarizona.com/
https://www.wholisticarizona.com/wholisticfinance

A former elementary teacher and museum education director, Rebecca operates Wholistic Finance in Tucson, AZ which she & her Acupuncturist husband Ron Chandler use to support their Wholistic Arizona Healing Ranch. Rebecca was a swimmer, ballet dancer, softball player, and B student through grade school and college. She sustained years of severe and often crippling depression, anxiety, and chronic illness from childhood into adulthood. She is grateful to share her story of transformation, finding her path to overall peace and relief. Rebecca's hope is to inspire confidence in others that they have a beautiful purpose here on earth, and that although this life sometimes brings insurmountable obstacles, we can find the power to overcome them when we lift our eyes to a wise, heavenly perspective. Our challenges prepare us to embrace our true power, which will fuel us to do the work we need to do here with more compassion.

WHEN I LEARNED TO PRAY

By Rebecca Chandler

Imagine you are the commander in a great battle.

You select your most loyal and strong as your starting troop to make significant headway, next you send in your valiant soldiers, and lastly you send your heaviest hitters, proven champions you can count on to finish the work needed. The opposition would always be trying to weaken your forces however they can, especially the most effective members of your team. As the battle escalates the opposition resorts to nastier, darker devices to undermine the resolve and power of your remaining warriors.

If you identify with the Me Too movement, you are among those heavy-hitting champion warriors sent to finish the battle. Only the battle isn't won with fighting or brutality, nor is it fought with weapons. This battle is a contest for goodness and light. It is not a battle of contention and anger, but one of kindness, charity, and love.

Our opposing side would have us lose hope, feel miserable and give up our power. Grief, sorrow, and distress are their aim for us. We, however, have protection through a nobler, superior power. While unseen, this power is the greatest influence we can call upon against opposition, even in the face of violation and extreme transgression.

We are being refined. And we have been selected to be here now. The experiences we have had that may be deemed "horrible" have a purpose. They are not easy. They are perhaps the hardest thing we'll ever be asked to undergo or overcome. But we *can* overcome them. We are the most valiant, the most competent, and the most reliable heroes in this era. We are also deeply, profoundly loved.

This refining is part of a process that prepares us for our future destiny and goals. We are warriors in a battle of trust, faith, dedication, and yielding our will to a higher vision, a greater purpose, and a more beautiful life. We are assured beautiful eternal rewards and great blessings when we submit in faithfulness and love to the plan and wisdom of this unseen protective influence. I learned to find, connect with and receive comfort from this influence when I learned to pray.

I bore my daughter, my first and only child, at 40 years old. I had not been a believer in much, maybe the concept of "the universe" or some ambiguous spiritual presence in the cosmos, but nothing formal, nothing I could connect with for comfort when pain occurred. When my daughter was two, my childhood anxiety returned in full force. I wasn't sure of the cause, but I was accustomed to its presence and discomfort and thought I could wait it out. By this time, I was already a regular patient in my husband's acupuncture and traditional medicine practice for pain, depression, and general wellness. We worked often on many phantom issues that bothered me consistently. This therapy brought much relief. As my healing advanced, I had the inspiration that I needed to begin trusting in things that I couldn't see. This brought me into a personal journey of finding truth that has strengthened my armor of faith, tested the limits of my resolve, and brought grace into my being as never before.

When this childhood anxiety collapse began occurring, I also found an amazing correspondence of silently receiving things that my heart secretly longed for. While material in nature sometimes, they were a charitable delivery of the desires of my heart by unseen angels. In one occurrence, I privately nurtured the desire for shearling boots, and then received a beautiful pair in my size and color in a bag of second-hand items from my neighbor's daughter to mine. Around the same time, my husband and I began searching for a church to establish a community for our growing family, and I met a new friend at our library's storytime. She introduced me to her friend with goats and homeschooling children, finally giving me a compatriot peer in a town I'd lived socially alone in for four years. Our new homeschooling and goat-owning friend introduced us to her church, which we joined after a year of sharing our lives and beliefs.

As I studied soul-satisfying beliefs and faith doctrine, I was taught how to pray. I didn't feel I knew God for sure, but I knew something was changing in me. I learned to call upon my Heavenly Father, thank Him, ask Him for what I desired or needed, and then close with thanks in the name of His son Jesus Christ. I practiced this pattern often. I began to feel different, better. My anxiety was still present, and I didn't want to leave the house very much except for necessities, but I was feeling more trust in things I couldn't see, yet knew were true.

Flash forward seven years. I had become much more outgoing and comfortable outside my home and my anxiety all but dissipated, allowing me to function better as a mom, wife, and community member. My family took small travels within our state as our vacations. We worked and homeschooled on our ranch. Our daughter was now 11 and a budding horsewoman. She had just been given a new horse, and it was living on a ranch three hours away in the mountains. Our generous neighbor loaned us an RV to camp at the ranch with the new horse. On Father's Day, we attended church service and went back to the RV to relax. We were all tired and thankful to head to bed early. At midnight, I woke up with a horrible searing pain in my hip. I shifted side to side with no relief. Then it came to me: *Pray*. I turned to my now reliable skill and began: "Dear Father in Heaven, I thank Thee. Please help me learn what Thou needest me to learn from this pain. I thank Thee. In the name of Jesus Christ. Amen."

I lay there for a short time trying to find relief by continuing to shift my weight and position. Then words came ringing in my conscience: *date rape drug*. I heard it several times in my head. I felt stunned. The pain diminished. As I lay there in our little RV camper in the mountains on a remote horse ranch in the middle of the quiet night, my eyes stared wide open into the darkness, hearing my own voice whisper in an echo of the words in my head: *date rape drug*.

I slept little until morning came. My mind and heart were in shock. I blankly functioned throughout the day, pouring over questions in my head, returning to prayer often to make sense of what I thought I was learning. Within two weeks, my understanding was fully opened to what I was shown that Father's Day.

Over the following eight months, I required much assistance and counseling to process and sort out my feelings and the facts. I regularly returned in my heart to the faith doctrines I learned in our church. There had to be a bigger purpose for going through what I learned had happened: that I had been an unconscious victim of repeated incest from 15 to 19 years old. During these adult months of recall, I had many flashbacks and memories from my youth that provided a clearer picture of behaviors and incidents that had previously puzzled, troubled, and perplexed me. I found healing through constant prayer, many tears, reading to understand the nature of this trauma, being still with my family on our home ranch, and many treatments in my husband's clinic for the shock my heart was now ready to confront.

One faith doctrine of our church helps me most in finding peace in my mind and heart. It is called the Plan of Happiness. In this Plan, we learn that we knew each other in the premortal, spirit world before we were born here into mortality. 2/3 of us each agreed to come, gain a body, experience trials, and follow the example of our Heavenly Father's son Jesus Christ to return to live with Heavenly Father when we pass from this life. Following the example of Jesus Christ entails enduring hard things, including pain at the hands of our peers, family, or others close to us, who we otherwise would expect to be our protectors, but who sometimes succumb to overwhelming addictions and personal pain that cause them to make unthinkable choices at our expense. 1/3 of the pre-mortal spirits chose not to follow the Plan and will never receive a body. They are the opposing team that pollutes pure desires and pushes innocent spirits toward nefarious actions that harm those of us who chose to follow the Plan. There was a war in Heaven when the third faction of spirits broke away from following the Plan. This war is in effect on earth today. We are the valiant, heavy-hitting fighters who chose to come here and represent all that is pure and light and do the most good while the world is at its darkest. The forces that oppose us would pull us down into darkness and misery. They would use us and abuse us, attempting to shadow our hearts with grief and anger.

In this Plan of Happiness, we agreed to endure in patience, learning to overcome our mortal and natural reactions to bodily harm and emotional pain, by seeing with divine eyes how this invasive experience could grow in us God-like qualities of kindness, tenderness, patience, charity, forgiveness, and compassion. If we complete our work here on earth without succumbing to that darkness and misery, no matter what horror is inflicted upon our bodies and spirits, then we will be doing the job we were sent here to do. We are not to go through this without help. We do not have to endure these pains and trials on our own, or only with our own strength. We can call **in prayer** upon all heavenly forces to help us, comfort us, strengthen us, relieve us, rebuild us, purify us, and repair us.

We are the valiant closers, sent here at this time to finish the best work on earth: to develop our strengths and use our nurturing capacities to bring healing to the hearts of others who suffer, lifting hands that hang down, feeding, clothing, and sheltering the abandoned. We are the ones God could count on. Even if we don't remember Him. He remembers us. He will send us the reinforcements of hope and comfort we need when we call to Him… when we cry out to Him… when we turn our whole souls to Him in our time of need. He will grow in us something we could never have developed ourselves. He will grow in us giant oak trees of massive charitable power. He will grow around us impenetrable armor of right thinking, virtuous speaking, compassionate serving, and loving kindness.

If you and I are the final team of warriors to complete the battle of light versus dark, we must have an enormous capacity to become kind. This Me Too experience is the melting away of our own strengths so that we may take on power beyond our mortal capacity by yielding ourselves to our maker, to God, and to the love of His son Jesus Christ. This is the time in the world when we can access miraculous, healing, heavenly power through praying to know who we are and to feel redeeming love like never before. We can be healed, and we can become healing helpers to any others who need us. When we let this trial refine us into the best of our potential, we are fulfilling our part of the Plan of Happiness.

I want to become the best of my possible potential. You can too. This is the way God provided, and that we agreed to before we came here, for us to become our best selves and to do the most good here. Turn to Him. He will show you who you are. He will help you feel your power, your potential, your proof that you are beloved and so needed on His team. You are a proven champion He knew He could depend on. When you are ready, let Him know through prayer. And He will fill your heart with divine love that will erase all pain and will fill you with the desire to go out and do more good! Let's go! I am here with you. And so is He.

Rebecca Chandler
Owner, Wholistic Arizona Healing Ranch

Jaime Lynne

Intuitive Thought Leader | Warrior of the light

https://www.instagram.com/sharpgirl79/
https://www.facebook.com/sharpgirl79

Jaime Lynne is a warrior of the light, an inspirational thought leader, and passionate about nature, photography, holistic wellness, and gourmet cooking.

Through her own life experience as a creative, US Veteran, wife, and mother, Jaime has become a change agent for women; liberating them to stand in their power and speak their truth—unapologetically.

In her own healing and self-discovering journey, Jaime has experienced such pivotal issues as judgment, guilt, blame, shame, and anger.

She aspires to elevate the conditioning around the old societal blueprint of women; sharing her gifts of intuitive energetic healing, including enhancing a deeper authentic connection with friends, family, work, and most importantly, the one you have with yourself.

She serves as a voice for trauma survivors by lifting the veil of silence—inspiring women to take back the authority of her own life and become her own she-ro.

She empowers women to open their wings and soar.

BIRD SET FREE

By Jaime Lynne

We met on a sunny autumn day on my military base in Germany. He was very charming. After a month of phone chatting, we set a date to see each other again.

It happened to be a winter night on the Autobahn. En route to his base, a few hours away from mine, I was in good spirits. I drove this road on many occasions and felt confident since I was a seasoned driver and have driven in a wide range of climate conditions.

However, a couple of hours into my drive, my confidence gradually diminished. An uneasiness crept into my soul as the fog drastically minimized my visibility.

It felt like I was moving through billowy clouds. The headlights aided me in some moments when I could see the obscured road. As an expert driver, I began to become more alert and cautiously continued to respond according to what was just faintly visible—and like a pilot, I began to trust my senses and fly by instrument—as the patchy mist began to thicken.

Technology was not so advanced yet; GPS and cell phones were nearly non-existent. It was just me and my trusty accordion fold-up map.

Growing up on the East Coast, I was used to driving in harsh snowy winters. However, being an American in a foreign land and knowing only a few phrases in German was considerably different.

I was at the mercy of my senses as I continued to move along the road, and the conditions worsened. The ominous thick fog closed in and surrounded my vehicle, suffocating my senses since I could only see about four feet ahead. As the snow started to frame the edges of the road, my intuition prodded me to seek guidance and ensure I was headed in the right direction.

I pulled into a gas station and saw police officers inside. YES! They must speak English and can help me! They reassured me that I was headed in the right direction. The only thing on my mind was to get to safety at my date's base.

I continued towards my destination on the Autobahn. I passed flashing signs, and suddenly the yellow-flashing lights were mere seconds away from my bumper! Before I had a chance to respond, I found myself gliding on what felt like a sleek sheet of ice.

I desperately attempted to maneuver the vehicle by turning my steering wheel and pumping my brakes, however, they were completely unresponsive. I slipped into a suspended motion. It felt like an eternity—and all I could do was agonizingly witness the near-fatal scene at a funeral's pace.

I slid off the road and rammed into a trailer hauling a cement cylinder and then twisted like an ice skater into a double axel. My face felt like it exploded as the airbag violently blew up in my face and thrust my head backward, slamming into the headrest as I watched my world tumble, twist, and turn with the momentum.

I experienced terror screeching in motion as I watched my world flip upside-down continuously as the shrieking inside my head deafened any other sound.

Finally, everything came to a halt.

Adrenaline pushed through my body like a dam broke. My vehicle seemed like a crushed tin can, and a flood of urgency surged through me to get out in case it caught fire.

As I fled the heap of piled metal, I caught sight of a masculine silhouette rapidly approaching me. As he drew closer, he reached out his hand to help me and I noticed the distinctive sleeve of his uniform. I quickly glanced around at the other familiar faces and recognized that they were the police officers who assisted me.

Amid the pandemonium, my excruciating migraine, and disorientation—the ambulance arrived and all I heard was the shrill of my pain and garbled German from the medics. I was so shaken up that I refused to accept help.

Distraught, I just wanted to get to safety and insisted on contacting my date. I trusted that he would come to my rescue.

I felt shattered, as my body felt like it was in pieces. The pain sliced through me and radiated down throughout my entire body and the deafening ringing in my ears echoed through my whole being. The police reluctantly concurred and proceeded to take me to the station, as they shared a universal look of horror and concern.

Horror-stricken, I saw what the policeman observed. It was a face that I didn't recognize staring back at me. I just stared at my reflection in the bathroom mirror, petrified.

My left eye was sunken in, I had bruises and swollen hematomas that were striking. I had a contusion across my hairline, a huge lump on the back of my head, and my left shoulder was so painful that I was hardly able to lift it up to inspect the rest of my injuries.

I looked down and noticed that the violent jolting, crashing, and thrashing caused the seatbelt to cut like a razor through my light blue blouse and jeans. The only thought repeating through my mind was, "I just want to get to safety."

At my base, it felt like everyone around me were like brothers and sisters. Surely, my date would be the same, or so I thought.

Shaken, I used their telephone to call my date and strained to see because I also developed a sensitivity to light. My date answered, obviously annoyed. He explained that he was drinking and would come with a friend to pick me up from the station.

Shocked and speechless, I lay across a row of chairs in the police station, warmed by my leather coat that I covered myself with like a blanket.

I felt myself drifting in and out of consciousness. Time passed until he finally arrived.

I walked outside and into the navy-blue sedan. The piercing pain of the bright early sun stabbed through my temples. I couldn't wait to just lie down, close my eyes, and rest.

When we arrived at his dormitory room, I asked him when he could bring me back to my base. Weak and impaired, I collapsed on his bed to rest. I felt him pressing his body on top of me. Trapped, I could barely see with the severe inflammation around my eyes as the overhead light caused me excruciating pain. I shut my eyes.

I smelled the scent of whiskey that permeated the air as he replied, "Before I take you anywhere, you're going to give me something first!"

I felt gut-wrenching nausea take over, warning me of the danger I was in. My tormentor was like a bird of prey.

Pinning me down with his dominant force, I was powerless and in agony from the accident. I felt that I had no choice except to comply as he started stripping off my clothes against my will. I mustered to push his body off mine as I said "No!" repeatedly. My head whipped back and forth as he continued violating me. All I could do was just lay there, in his grip and with nowhere to go. Shards of pain ripped through me inside and out. I was helpless. It was just a silent scream. At that moment, I knew no one was coming to my rescue.

In the several weeks following my traumatic incidents, I found myself healing alone in my dormitory room weighted down with heavy medication, and healing from a severe concussion. People stopped by to check in on me, brought meals, and briefly visited, but for the most part, I was left with myself and plenty of unwanted time to reflect.

When I regained awareness of what happened, the reality of being raped hit me like a ton of bricks. My voice and my dignity were viciously ripped out of me.

As I lay there alone with my convulsive self-deprecating thoughts, my emotions began to build turbulence like a roller coaster hurling off its tracks. Shame climbed up to the top of the hill as blame followed it down. It was the beginning of the brutal cycle of emotional rape.

Back-to-back trauma felt to me like a centrifugal force; each jerk of my self-sabotaging thoughts tumultuously turned into one of self-judgment, twisting into tormenting memories, and tumbling into exhaustion. It felt like a torturous nightmare and all the shrieking scenes and fearful emotions that came with it.

I felt an overwhelming sense of guilt over my decision to go visit him in the first place. Then the rise of a storm surged within me where the downpour of tears seemed to be endless.

A rage of fury followed— towards myself and then towards the attacker who raped me.

I felt so alone. I was the one who was always the hero for others and now I needed someone to be that for me and I didn't know how to ask for help. What would I say? How could anyone help me or understand what I was going through? Then, self-doubt flooded in, and I would ask myself, "What if no one believes me, even if I decide to tell someone?"

When I was in the armed forces, an unspoken shield of protection was often formed for things that didn't shine on the military in a positive light. It was a common understanding that things of this nature were swept under the rug. It was a well-known culture in the military during this time that highly invested soldiers were rarely found guilty of crimes, especially of sexual assault or sexual misconduct.

I made the excruciating decision to stay silent to protect myself and not get others involved. I kept myself caged up for so long, continuing to appear strong, but it was just a facade. Truthfully, I was hypersensitive to protecting myself from anything and anyone.

Weeks passed before I felt the courage to tell my story to a friend who consistently showed compassion and support to me. He kindly helped me feel heard and supported, and we built a strong bond. I was terrified of being judged, but I followed my intuition and felt safe enough to share it with my entrusted friend. He emphasized that there was nothing I did or could have said that would make the sexual assault my fault.

I realized that sometimes we need to borrow the positive beliefs of how others see us until we can believe it for ourselves. My friend reminded me of how worthy I was and he shared the greatness of what he and so many others saw in me, and I eventually opened the latch to the cage I had been keeping myself trapped in. Being able to speak to him helped me sing my beautiful song, and by doing so, I discovered my own wings.

As I look back today, having the support of someone I knew that cared for me was what helped me to release the barrier of guilt and shame that I created within myself. It gave me the permission to surrender to heal my heart. That was when I felt open to trusting again.

I cherish the love and authenticity my friend poured into me through the most vulnerable time of my life. He valued me, and as a result, I learned how to value myself. This honorable friend is my husband. We continue our special closeness, and it has flourished over decades of joy and trust. Our relationship is priceless.

In the broken societal blueprint, it's taboo to discuss the subject of rape. This darkness needs to be brought into the light. In the years I have spent expressing my rape, so many women shared with me, in confidence, that they too were sexually assaulted and didn't tell anyone because they blamed themselves.

No one chooses or deserves to be sexually assaulted. NO means NO! Period.

Rape does not discriminate against race, age, or gender. If you have been a victim of sexual assault, you are not alone. We are survivors. We keep the trauma alive even when it is kept silent and hidden, giving the oppressor misplaced power, and feeling trapped permeates our lives. The heinous act is not the survivor's burden to carry.

Leadership coach and poet, Sean Smith, said, "Our wounds are somebody else's wings."

When we can speak our truth, healing is unleashed within us.

Know that what you've been through doesn't define you. The essence of who you are stands on an unshakable foundation when you release that latch on your cage.

Your voice is like the bird set free.

Open your wings and fly.

Isabelle Ruiz

Owner of Bellas Party & Crafts Boutique

https://www.facebook.com/authorisabelleruiz
https://www.facebook.com/bellaspartyncraftsboutique/
https://www.instagram.com/bellas_partyncrafts_boutique/

Mother & Wife, Student, Youth Sports Coach, Entrepreneur, Author and A woman who prays, slays, minds her business makes money and trusts God for the rest. Isabelle is a woman empowerment supporter and is an ambitious effervescent woman equipped to be an advocate for women and youth all over the world to not only inspire to speak their truth and find healing from their traumas but also empower youth and women to help build bravery and find their faith in God's purpose and to trust the power of prayer. Isabelle is on a mission to spread Sexual abuse awareness, a topic that isn't reiterated enough and is a survivor breaking the silence, giving the message that there is no disgrace in being a sexual abuse survivor.

I AM SEEN, I AM HEARD

By Isabelle Ruiz

I was about five years old when the sexual abuse began, and it went up until the age of 15 by three different men—a stepparent, and two step-uncles—while I was being raised by my grandfather and his wife. I did not realize what was being done to me was wrong. It felt wrong, but the understanding that was embedded in me was that it was a special little secret act of love that was kept between us and done behind the little casita out back. Until one day when my grandma walked in on a scene. I was about five years old and was lying on the couch with my pants down while this uncle was looking down at me fondling his privates and explaining to me how he would never hurt me and telling me to remember not to say anything. He was about to rape me. My grandmother beat him up and threw him out. She then showered me, sat me down, and explained how this is something that never needs to be talked about again and that I needed to forget it as if it never happened.

I can't explain to you the type of sadness that was in me. I missed my mom so much. She was living in the states and I was in Mexico, and I know my family in Mexico loved me in their own way, but I was treated differently. There was some sort of grudge towards me. I knew it as a kid, and it felt like I wasn't loved. Feeling like such a burden made me want my mom more.

I remember sitting outside washing laundry and hanging it out on the clothesline and just talking up to the sky. I thought maybe my words would travel and my mom would hear them somehow and hear my plea and cries. I would pray that she would just bring me home with her already. I wanted my mom terribly. Then finally, she decided to bring me back to the states with her. I was eight years old when her husband began his grooming and his threats: "Don't say anything, it's our secret, and I'll give you whatever you want," or" if you say something I will kill your mom," or "don't cry, its better you than your sisters right?" Let me tell you, any little thing that me and my sisters did bad meant that we would get beat, and he would say, "I'll make sure not to spank you so hard, but you have to be my good girl that I taught you to be." For every little thing, any little outburst, I was brought into that bathroom where I was given two choices: get spanked or let myself be touched/do the touching and be taught to be a "good girl." That is when I started to question what the heck was going on. But if I said anything, my sisters would be in danger, or my mom would be in danger, so I must remain a "good girl" for them so that they can continue to be safe. I'm the oldest so it's my job to protect my siblings, and it's up to me to ensure my mom stays safe. I had to keep the secret safe, and in the same way, I must keep my loved ones safe. He would come into our room almost every night, and I would have to pretend I was sleeping. I couldn't face what was happening to me awake, otherwise, he would make me do the touching. I would be so scared waiting every night, staring at the doorknob because I knew that at any moment it was going to turn or he would pick the lock open and let himself in. I always hated sleeping on the edge of the bed, but having my sisters up against the wall relieved me because he wouldn't get to them. When he would be done pleasing himself and leave, I would run to lock the door again and just sit in the closet and cry and pray he wouldn't come back. I thought: should I wait for him to fall asleep so I can kill him in his sleep? But there was no way I could be strong enough, no way I could leave my siblings fatherless and take away my mom's love from her.

As I got a little older, I started to have flashbacks to when I was in my toddler years, and I started to remember that this man that my mother was with wasn't in the picture before. Aside from that, I started to understand that what was happening wasn't right, I know for sure now. A lot isn't right here; who is this man really? How come I can't remember him clearly? Why would a father do this? How can I get rid of him? I started to feel disgusting, and that's when the questions began flowing even more. I started by asking my mom if this man was my father. I had gone through the birth certificates, and he's not on mine— why? Of course, I knew why, but I wanted so badly for my mom to tell me. Of course, she didn't tell me. Instead, it was "Isabelle you are his daughter, I would never lie to you, and you are just being crazy." I needed the truth to come from her, even though I already knew it. I felt that with her honesty, I would be able to build up the courage to tell her what she thought her beloved, amazing husband was doing to me. But I couldn't. I was just being crazy, and besides, *everyone* loved him. He was this great person in everyone's eyes. No one was going to believe a coming-of-age adolescent that is confused, lost, hurt, lonely, and more than anything a rebellious teen, and a liar.

In my mind, I thought "Well, my sisters aren't being harmed. They would tell me or I would see something." I asked them so many times if they were ever touched (and they were always too scared to tell me the truth). To add to that thought, I also didn't want my mom to be hurt.

My mother became so invested in building her career and her self-image that it led her to addiction. She was never home, and when she was she wasn't really there. I couldn't talk to her. Everything was always a bother, and I felt so closed in with no one to talk to. I wanted someone to help me. I wanted to be able to put a stop to what was happening. Until one day, I just got so fed up and tired of him and what he was doing because he just always wanted more. I felt like at any moment I was going to be laying on that couch again and no one was going to save me this time around. It finally sparked in me, and I realized I was the only one going to be able to protect myself. I finally stood up to him and said no, no more, and he looked me in the eyes as he grabbed me by the throat and said "No one will ever believe you. Everyone knows what a liar you are. You are here because I want you here, not your mom. No one loves you. No one is going to love you, and if you keep this up soon you won't even have your mom or your siblings." The rage in me grew so much at that moment. I pushed him away and then it quickly escalated as I told him I would be speaking up. It turned into a very bloody fight. My mom came running up asking what was going on. That is when the truth finally came out. I threw in my mom's face my pain, my hurt, and everything that he was doing to me. I let out how much I hated her for lying to me and not telling me the truth about him not being my real father. I will never forget the look of disappointment on her face. She was not surprised, and looked like she wished she didn't have me— like she hated me.

Once things calmed down, she sat me down and tried to tell me that I have a mental problem and am bipolar, and the things I'm saying are "trauma dreams," things that I think are happening because I'm re-living and "imagining" the things that happened when I was small. She asked me how could I say things like this when I wear short clothing, and that someone that wears short clothing isn't someone being sexually abused. I knew then that she was always going to choose him, and she was always going to have his back. She then proceeded to tell me that she will be sending me away with her aunts so that I can be a free child and have a chance at a normal upbringing. She said that another reason why I'm speaking out and lying about such horrific things is because they were strict. That their strictness was what was giving me the motive to say those "lies." That it was only because I wanted the freedom to do what all the other teens were doing. The only reason that man was strict was because he didn't want me to be comfortable with anyone. He alienated me so that I wouldn't feel comfortable speaking up. Right there, I felt it in my stomach. I failed my sisters and caused them to be left alone and vulnerable. I hated myself. At that moment, I regretted never following through with the thoughts of killing him in his sleep. My sisters assured me nothing was happening to them, and when I looked back at it, I was so stupid to believe that he had them so scared.

So, what happened after that? They cut off all communication between my sisters and me. The fear of standing together and seeking help was just too much of a risk. My mother was not going to let him go, and nothing and no one is going to take him from her no matter what she had to lose. Honestly, I did believe my sisters at the time. He was good at lurking and doing his deeds in the shadows. I never once saw him look at my sisters the way he did at me. I did believe they were his real daughters as well; I thought that he wouldn't do this to his own blood, and that is why it would only be me he was doing this to. So, I wasn't given a choice, and my mother's solution was to send me away.

At 15 years old the next chapter of my life began in Leavenworth, Washington. My mom flew me away to "Timbuktu," which was such a culture shock for me coming from the big Las Vegas, Nevada. Man, my poor aunts, they did not deserve any of the things I put them through either. They welcomed such an angry, resentful, and very hateful young woman. My mind had shut down and was unwilling to accept that I could be loved at all. If my mom did not want me, then how could anyone ever love me? I heard "with that attitude and character you will be alone all of your life" and "No one could ever love someone so full of attitude and anger" a lot growing up. The worst part is that I believed it, and my mission was to drive my aunts crazy enough so they would send me back to my mom. Even though I was hurt and angry at my mom, that was all I wanted, to be where she and my siblings were. I wanted so badly for my Washington family to be fed up with me so I could be sent back. When I did go back, I was about to be 17. Then, one day something happened, and my sister finally spoke up and told me the things that our stepfather did to her too. In that moment, everything came crashing down inside me. I felt like it was my fault. If I had always been that "good girl" this would not have happened to her too. After pulling it together, I called the police and told them everything. They then took us to the family court to write out statements and investigate. They screwed up big time when they put us in a room alone with my mom right from the start and then heard from my mom about how rebellious and hateful and bipolar I was. The look they gave was not reassuring. I wasn't in a safe place, and I knew they weren't going to believe me. My mother could sell ice to an Eskimo, she is always so believable. She took advantage of the love we have for her to protect this man. She told us we would grow up and have our own lives one day, and that she will be alone. She asked us to please not do this to her, to please lie and say we were just traumatized from what happened to us when we lived in Mexico because they (my sisters) also suffered sexual abuse there and it was kept in secret from everyone. She said that if we lie, she will make sure this man never comes into our lives again and we will never have to see him and that she would ensure to get him help, so please be forgiving and have mercy for her sake.

I felt this overwhelming guilt. I knew that I failed my sisters and was so sorry I didn't protect them. At that moment I owed everything to them and felt like everything was my fault. As I talked to them, all they could say was that they were scared. They didn't want to lose their dad and put him in jail for the rest of his life, and they were scared my mom would try and commit suicide. You see, she made it clear that she needed him to survive and that without him she would be lifeless. So, we lied for her. They sent us back home and nothing was done. I called the police and asked for help for nothing.

My mom left that night in the middle of the night to start over in a different city with him and his biological children and left my sisters and me behind. I was able to be on my own, but my sisters went into foster care. My mother never looked back at what she left here in Vegas. Well, I never looked back on it after that either. He was far away from us now and will never be able to hurt us anymore. What could we do now but keep on living? The worst has already happened and now the best is yet to come. Since that day, it was never talked about again.

Having to face the people who sexually abused you when you were a child is an everyday reality for so many people, and it's not talked about enough. Now that I am older, I can see why I have so much trouble communicating and expressing my feelings properly. I have problems trying to communicate when I am angry or sad. I was taught to not show emotion, and I was to be seen and not heard, because if I did then I was unappreciative, crazy, or just flat-out bipolar and mental. If I cried, I would get yelled at because "What am I crying for? You have such a good life." I was the kid and they were the adults, and children are to be seen and not heard; I had no voice because I was a child. It really explains why I am quick to lash out instead of being able to talk and have a healthy and proper discussion.

I am, however, a daily work in progress, and with prayer, experience, and wisdom I have gotten so much better. I have always said my story belongs in a book for women like me to read and know *me too—*, you are not alone. It's important to me to spread awareness and help young people and adults to speak up and let it out. Break the cycles of not letting our children have a voice. I am a mom of four beautiful children, and I am always encouraging them to not only stand up for themselves but also to be brave enough to stand and speak for those that don't have the courage to do it for themselves yet. They have a clear understanding of what is right and wrong and that their voice matters.

They that child sexual abuse is a social injustice that is given some of the least attention. It's not talked about enough in schools, and our youth need more help now than ever. Everyone must understand that sexual harassment behavior needs to be brought to attention. It starts with our youth. Boys and girls need to understand that certain boundaries can't be crossed. Even if television makes it seem normal, it's not, and we need to be more vocal about it so that when we have the opportunity to help people recover from abuse, we understand that it requires time, strength, and support. Victims need support from family, the community, and mental health services, and they need access to resources and a safe person. It may be difficult, but it is important to notify law enforcement if anyone discloses sexual abuse. I can't stress this enough— BELIEVE your children when they are uncomfortable with a specific adult and support them. This is so important and keeps them safe. This subject needs to be reiterated over and over and discussed publicly so that those who suffer silently for many years can overcome this trauma.

Sometimes my journey is overwhelmingly challenging. I get caught up in the struggle and forget that I have overcome the worst parts. I forgive as our sins have been forgiven, but I will never forget, and I will always be working on my healing process. It's never ending, and I always have triggers, but I love me, and I should've always known my worth and should've never accepted that I couldn't speak up. Children are to be SEEN and HEARD. There's a little girl in me who has started growing up all over again, but this time it's different. This time she is heard. She is not crazy— she is strong enough to say I am worthy. I am no longer ashamed to share my story. God has given me his love, mercy, and glory and has helped me build the courage to say "Me too, but never again!" That is all I will ever need. I am SEEN and I am HEARD. Thank you God!

Nicole Curtis

Executive Assistant to the CEO of She Rises Studios

https://www.facebook.com/nicolecurtissherisesstudios
https://www.instagram.com/nicolecurtis_sherisesstudios/
https://www.sherisesstudios.com/
https://www.facebook.com/groups/sherisesstudioscommunity

Speaker, Author, and Mentor. Nicole is a tenacious woman geared to serving and helping women grow, elevate and succeed in life and in business. Nicole's mission is to not only educate and empower women, but she also specializes in building true authentic professional relationships with women all over the world. She loves to support and guide women in business to become more visible worldwide and she is a mental health advocate for moms with struggling children.

HELPING WOMEN HEAL FROM CHILD SEXUAL ABUSE

By Nicole Curtis

This chapter is dedicated to all the women Child Sexual Abuse (CSA) warriors who, despite the shit we have gone through, continue to fight. For the CSA women that are struggling to fight, please know I am here for you and that you aren't in this alone!

First, I want these women to know they are incredible and beautiful! I know that you might not always believe this—goodness there are times when I don't! I have days where a trigger will set me off into such a downward spiral that I am instantly brought right back to that time in my life when I was a vulnerable little girl who didn't understand what was happening but knew deep down it was wrong.

Experiencing horrific trauma such as CSA isn't something we will ever forget. It is something that we battle and face every day whether we are feeling good or not. We will never be able to erase what happened to us, but we sure as hell can write the next chapter in our life!

It is time, CSA warriors, to unite and help our CSA sisters that are struggling and feel as if they are alone. Let's help lift them up with love and support. Let's band together because when we do we are stronger.

I am writing this chapter because I want to help you, dear reader, who is struggling with silencing the voices in your head that are telling you that you are dirty, worthless, alone, and exposed. I know they can get loud, almost to the point you're so broken down you feel helpless, hopeless, and lost. Believe me, I've felt this way before!

These voices echoed in my head for years. They were there when I was going through my abuse as a little girl and continued to get louder as the years went on. See, for so long I, too, believed that I was dirty; that no one could ever really love me because I was no longer pure. A piece of me was forever taken and no matter what I said or did I was never going to get it back. I felt worthless because a piece of my soul was stolen from me. Every day I felt numb, alone, and empty inside! Each day was a struggle just to hold my head above water so I wouldn't drown in a pool of darkness, and some days when the voices were screaming I had thoughts of what it might be like if I just stopped treading water.

I hated the fact I was violated. My voice was silenced and my words didn't mean anything. I was so helpless and terrified back then, and it pains me to know that my mind, body, and soul were taken advantage of and left exposed to a person who dared to call himself a religious family man. He was a joke, but guess what— the joke was on him. Because *he didn't win*. I am a strong, brave, unstoppable woman who knows her worth and value, and I live my life as my most powerful self every single day! What he did to me no longer has a hold on me and it never will again.

I know that the Child Sexual Abuse you experienced, dear reader, isn't exactly like mine, but you and I have shared similar thoughts and feelings. Today I want to help you rewrite those feelings because what happened to you wasn't your fault. Let me say that again! The abuse that happened to you wasn't your fault!

I want to share with you three key concepts that have helped me in my healing journey that I continue to implement in my life today because my journey isn't over! I continue to fight, and every day I write what happens next in my life.

1. I took all of my ugly thoughts and hurtful feelings and came to terms with the fact that what was done to me was something I didn't have control over. Therefore, I had to stop hating myself for them. There came a point in time when I had to stop focusing on what happened to me and begin focusing on what I wanted to see happen in my life. Here is an exercise that I

started doing in my mid 20s when I first began my journey of healing that helped shape me into the woman I am today!

**Take a piece of paper, write your name in the middle of it, and then circle your name. Then start branching lines off your name and write down any words, thoughts, or phrases that you think of when you ask yourself this question: What kind of woman do I want to be in a year? Whatever you write down, make it happen. When I did this for myself, much of what I wrote down I had no idea how to start making happen. So, I started to seek out the answers. I asked for professional help, found women to mentor me, and spent a lot of time researching and studying.

2. I accepted all the parts of me that I believed were damaged mentally, physically, and spiritually and began to rewire them. Meaning I had to change how I talked to myself and what I believed about myself. I learned how to create boundaries for myself and others around me. I created a deeper relationship with myself by not only confronting my fears but establishing personal principles of self-love and self-worth in my daily life!

   Exercise: Look at yourself in the mirror, smile, wrap your arms around yourself (big hug) and say the words "I love you" out loud while you look at yourself. I know this sounds crazy and stupid, but doing this exercise helped me. It helped me not only start believing in myself, but I also began to fall in love with myself. It helped me start breaking down the walls of not feeling loved or worthy, dirty, and alone. I started to become my own best friend.

3. I took responsibility for how I was treating myself. This one was a big one for me because of the abuse I endured. I carried so much hurt, pain, and brokenness inside of me that I began

to take it out on myself. I wasn't just saying mean things to myself, I was damaging my body because I started down the path of an eating disorder. I became a heavy binge eater. I would go two to three days barely eating anything and then boom I would eat non-stop for two to three days. This vicious cycle continued for years. I used it as a coping mechanism to help me try and block out what happened to me and what I was feeling. When I began taking responsibility for the harm I was inflicting on myself I began to redirect my binge eating. Taking responsibility made me 1) come to terms that it wasn't my body's fault for the abuse, and 2) start to do different things instead of binging. I would go for a walk in the woods instead, or head to the beach, listen to music, call a close friend or family member, spend time with my dog, or go for a drive.

**Exercise: I want you to create a list of three to five positive activities that you can begin doing if you are using some kind of self-destruction to cope with your abuse. I want you to use this list as a guide so when you get that urge to be destructive, you can replace it with something healthier. The more you implement this the more you will begin to see that your brain will start rewiring your need to self-destruct. Give this a try for 28 days and let me know how it goes. If you decide to add more positive activities to your list, go for it! The more the merrier!

My hope in sharing these three concepts with you is that they help you as they have helped me. What happened to you and what you have gone through doesn't have to define you! Your life isn't over, I promise! You are a powerful woman who deserves to live the life she wants to live, and it's time that you start believing it.

We are warriors, no longer victims!

We are Me Too But Never Again!!!

Madison Clark

Desert Pups LLC -Madison Tanner Media - Copywriting
Dog Daycare

www.instagram.com/themaddieclark
https://www.linkedin.com/in/madison-tanner-hunter-clark/
www.desertpups.com

Madison Tanner Clark is the founder of doggy daycare chain Desert Pups and a professional copywriter born and raised in Miami, Arizona.

When she was 18, she moved to New York City for her undergraduate in Media, Culture, and the Arts. There she worked as a stage manager for several off-Broadway productions and spent most of her time at a local doggy daycare which Desert Pups is inspired by. Upon graduation, she moved to Las Vegas to go full-throttle in her writing and social media career.

Now Madison has her own writing company where she helps bloggers, marketing agencies, and influencers with their copy to continue writing her own books. Her daycare is now open where she currently resides in Phoenix, Arizona with her fur baby, Hollywood.

DEFY IMPOSSIBLE CIRCUMSTANCES

By Madison Clark

To my brothers, thank you for being my guardian angels and protecting me through everything.

Regardless of anything that has happened to me, I have always been a happy and resilient child. Nothing stopped that— not even sexual abuse.

Sexual abuse does not discriminate against race, age, or gender. It's one of those things you can watch all day long on Law and Order, but can't fathom talking about in reality. You can read it as a news notification on your phone and be unphased, but tangle your words up if someone were to confide in you. We as a society do not take sexual abuse lightly, but do we understand the repercussions of making it trendy whilst *attempting* to spread a message?

The "Me Too" movement was intense for a lot of people, myself included. I felt anger as people made light of it. I was saddened by the stories of others. I felt conflicted if I should share mine. Then I did, and I'm doing it again.

Being molested as a young child is something no one prepares you for, whether you are the child or parent. No one warns you that over 80 percent of the time the abuser is someone you know and trust. I hate talking about it, but not because of obvious reasons. I don't want to be seen as a victim or a survivor.

I hate that term: survivor. It makes it seem like I fought my way out of a life-threatening situation. I didn't do that. I was a baby. There was nothing to escape from. It was, unfortunately, life as I knew it.

The abuse came from my babysitter's husband, aka Nana and Tata.

Nana knew about it. She stood by him when he was in court. She pretty much said "I told you so," when there wasn't enough proof against him, and he was deemed not guilty. She allowed it to happen in her own home with half a dozen babies and a few preteens at his disposal—and he used every single one of us—some more than others, some more aggressively than others. Albeit, in the late 90s computers were not a normal commodity in every home just yet. Tata used that to his advantage as he enticed us with computer games like solitaire and pinball. But, as our eyes and brains were distracted by the flashing lights and excitement on the screen, little did we truly realize what was happening with our bodies.

He made us feel special while she made us and our parents feel safe. Maybe that's why it was so hard for any of us to think that something sinister was lurking in the nearby shadows. Sometimes he would have us all stand in a line, wait our turn, and take turns sitting on his lap as he was on the computer. Other times he would single us out and we would feel chosen or jealous—depending on if we were picked or not. We were brainwashed into the daily routine of playing computer games with Tata so much so that sometimes we were the ones to ask him to play games.

We were raised to not think much of how Tata would wear just his underwear around the house. We were told to turn away from the TV if anything sexually explicit was happening. Adult Madison questions that now, "Why are you playing that for kids?" We had movies turned all the way up when Tata was in his bedroom. Why? Adult Madison knows why now. Us littles were not allowed on the big bed for any reason, but the preteens were.

Sometimes during nap time we would hear screaming and one of the preteen girls would be crying coming out of Nana and Tata's bedroom. If we got up during that time, Nana would lure us into the kitchen with homemade buttered tortillas and that is where she taught me how to get really good at deflecting.

The day I spoke up to my parents is when I witnessed something really bad between him and the preteen girl mentioned above. I was lucky for many reasons, but the biggest one was that my parents believed me and supported me. However, the justice system did nothing for me or my abused peers. They didn't believe us because we were *just* children and children make up stories all the time, right? Besides, how could such a well-known name in our small town be accused of such a heinous crime? The detective on the case was new to town and didn't understand that one couldn't easily take down someone with his name. That same detective ended up killing himself once he realized he couldn't do anything to help us or himself.

My parents did all they could to right this wrong, and frankly, they did their best. Mom and Dad, thank you for never allowing me to become a victim, for teaching me how to defy my circumstances, and for never allowing anyone other than myself to define my future.

I was in a brutal car accident in 2020 and had a lot of pain in my neck and shoulders. I was referred to a chiropractor—who was a great man and did not do anything to harm me, by the way. On my first visit, I felt confusion, tears welling up, and my skin becoming hot and fragile as he worked on my upper body. A woman later came in to do a massage on my shoulders. I had to steady my breathing so as to not go into a full-fledged panic attack. The moment I got home from the appointment, I threw up multiple times and sat in the shower as I sobbed while considering smashing my head against the marble wall to ease my mental pain.

I physically can't let anyone touch my neck and shoulders, especially men. I play off my involuntary response of jumping away by nervously laughing and saying that I am simply extremely ticklish there. But I'm not ticklish at all - which is a trauma response. Go figure.

Bless my father's heart, he used to grab me by the shoulders and squeeze me lovingly as a kid. It was his way of showing love to his daughter whom he'd written off as a tomboy and not affectionate. I would flinch in pain. Eventually, he learned to stop. He thought he was hurting me physically. He didn't realize the mental pain it took on me instead.

That is where *he* would touch us when we were specially chosen.

At this point, it has been over 20 years since the abuse. Only one person, my first love, has ever touched my shoulders without me having a reaction. The moment I realized this, my body celebrated this achievement by fainting for the first time ever and throwing up on him. I have him to thank for literally holding my hand through some of those hard, traumatic barriers I had to cross.

Although I still struggle with intimacy and trusting people, (because who doesn't these days?) I think I came out of that abusive situation relatively unscathed and without a victim mentality.

I have my parents to credit for that. My mother raised me to have a voice for those without one and to never let anyone get the final say as to how I am living my life. My father taught me that justice isn't always fair, but that God has a way of evening out the score eventually. They both told me, "All of the shit you've gone through? It's not for nothing, Mad Dog. You'll understand one day."

Man, don't you hate it when your parents are right?

Parents, believe your children when they have a bad feeling about someone. They are a lot more in-tune with things than most educated adults are. Don't become a helicopter parent and never let your child leave the house, but stay aware. Keep your mind open to your children, and for the love of God, do not think anyone is immune to trustworthy, wholesome-looking monsters like Tata.

To the kids who were in my shoes, are in my shoes, and will be in my shoes—you are not at fault for this.

No matter what is explicitly told to you or manipulated to seem otherwise, this is not your fault. Please never utter the words, "I wish I knew why they did that to me." Because you don't want to know why. You really don't want to see the inner workings of a disgusting excuse of a human. They want you to see the darkness and to be in the darkness with them.

I challenge you to be the light. Be the brightness that illuminates every bad thought, memory, and experience that has embedded itself into you. Burn so bright that you blind them from their dark ways and they have no choice but to see your sunny, bright face. They wanted to dim your future, but instead, you are a dazzling ray of hope and resilience.

No one is allowed the power to take your future away from you. My future is mine, not his. Your future is yours, and yours alone.

Divya Chandegra

Life & Wellness Soul Guide

https://www.facebook.com/Life-and-Wellness-with-Divya-115873590689176
https://www.instagram.com/divya.chandegra/
https://www.divya-chandegra.com/
https://www.divya-chandegra.com/subscribe

Divya Chandegra is a life and wellness guide and soul coach. Her mission in life is to empower mums and female professionals to heal their limiting childhood beliefs and subconscious blocks to free themselves and future generations from repeating patterns that keep them trapped in cycles, through conscious decision-making and conscious living.

She has developed an online program based on her 3-step A.I.R framework enabling clients to fast-track their self-mastery within 7 days by focusing on their inner child, generational patterns, mindset reprogramming, self-care, and unconditional love.

For more on living a balanced life in alignment with your Soul, access her free Understanding Your Inner Child mini-course on her website.

"She is brave and courageous - the woman one who chooses to love without conditions, for she knows that she has to re-visit her childhood to completely liberate her Self to find her way to Unconditional Love."
—Divya Chandegra

MOVING THROUGH MY FEARS FREED ME TO FIND MY SELF

By Divya Chandegra

"Sometimes asking for help also means you are helping yourself"
—Renuka Pitre

I'm 28 years old. A professional, working as a digital project manager for a leading agency in London. I work hard and the deadlines always loom. The hours aren't 9-5 like other professions. I meet a guy on a matrimonial dating site. He's educated. He's from a high caste. He's from a good family and he's an intelligent web developer who owns his own property and lives locally. My parents would approve. I'm intrigued by his intellect and he's surprised by mine. We're in the same industry, albeit in different disciplines. I understand his world—or so I thought.

Over the course of six months, we meet five or six times. I wouldn't call it dating as such. I've told my mum, but nobody else knows because he isn't a constant in my life. There's nothing to know. Except this…

Before it began

I'm at a friend's house, catching up when he calls. I can't take the call. He calls again and again. I message back, "I'm just at a friend's house chatting to aunty and uncle. I'll call you when I leave." He calls again. I answer and he switches on me.

There's no consideration, no respect — it's all about him. Basic human decency and courtesy no longer exist and every profanity comes out of his mouth. I politely say, "I think we should talk about this later," and cut the call.

I call back as soon as I leave my friend's house and find myself having to explain the situation. This doesn't feel good to me. What the hell is going on? I hardly know this guy. I don't need to explain myself to him. I tell him I don't think it's going to work between us.

And then it starts...

The unspeakable texts, the endless calls from unknown numbers. All day, all night. I can't sleep. I get up for work every day and pretend everything is okay. I can't switch off my phone at night because my alarm won't go off for work if I do, so I put it on silent. I try to rest, but it's on my mind constantly. During the day he calls from private numbers, and I answer by saying, "What do you want?" I know it's him. I'm exhausted and it's draining. I don't know who to turn to.

At the agency one day, I receive an SMS from what looks like my CEO saying inappropriate and disgusting things. He's using some kind of web tool where he customises the sender *name*. It goes on for weeks: The messages, the calls, the looking behind me to see if someone is following me. I feel unsafe and alone. I start collating a list of every message and call on a spreadsheet. It forms the basis of my evidence. There are over 200 line items.

I know it's time to report it, so I call the police. I explain the situation to a woman over the phone, and she mentions 'Madonna whore syndrome,' gives me a brief indication of what it is, and of course, I go and research the hell out of it. She tells me if I ever feel unsafe or threatened that I should call the police immediately and that this is serious.

A new start

An opportunity for a new job comes up. I take it and decide not to update my Linkedin profile because perhaps I can get away from this guy. I can change my number too. He still knows roughly where I live, but maybe I'd at least feel safer if he doesn't know where I work. The dread sits with me every day, and I worry for my parents' safety as well as my own. The guilt and shame are ever-present. I'm so tired.

I start the new job and feel slightly like I'm getting things under control, but then I get a call from a friend asking if I've seen my Facebook profile. I'm not very active on social media and had completely stopped using it since this all started. My friend stays on the phone with me and tells me to type my number or name into the search engine.

It's the last straw. I feel like I've been sucker punched. The shame, the distress, the dread. I begin solution-searching, so no one finds out. I screen grab the Facebook page because I need it for my evidence log. I report the page and within minutes Facebook takes the page down. Relief! Breathe…

The shadow pops up

He's created a fake profile by stealing my picture from my real profile, listing my family home address and my mobile number and is selling sexual services. Thinking about it now still makes my eyes well up. I was always taught to be tough, operating predominantly in my masculine energy, so I've been action and solutions focused, which perhaps served me well for this painfully traumatic ordeal. I still felt so alone. I was grateful for the heads-up from my friend.

I save the screenshot of the fake profile in my log. I check Facebook the next day and he's put another profile up. I screenshot it and report it again and it's taken down. I tell my new employer what's going on. It's the first time I've spoken about it out loud.

Moving on

It's a Saturday in the summer and I have plans to go to Bristol for the night with friends while my parents are away for a wedding. I'm vacuuming when the doorbell rings, but I don't hear it through the noise of the vacuum. My sister and brother call me down. The neighbour is at the door saying someone just smashed my car windows and slashed the tyres. The car is in the drive with the alarm going off.

I feel like everything is falling apart. There are children that play on the cul-de-sac! It's broad daylight on a Saturday! My neighbour explained that there was an Indian kid running away from my drive and that he tried to chase after the kid, but someone was waiting for him in a car and they sped off. The car was a dark Rover saloon, but he couldn't get the number plate.

I know who it is. I know that's his dad's car. He's dropped me round the corner in that car once.

I didn't think he'd be stupid enough to come to the street. It's easy to find my house on the street if you know my car — it's the only Audi cabriolet on the street.

Asking for help

> *"Be strong enough to stand alone, smart enough to know when you need help, and brave enough to ask for it"*
> —Anonymous

It was time. My sister and friend take me to the local police station and I report the grievance with a file full of evidence. I tell them his name and where he lives, and I assure them with 100% certainty that if they check his IP, they'll see that he created the fake profiles and is using some software to send customised and anonymous texts and calls. My parents and uncle warn me that if I press charges, it will all come out in court. I need to be brave and choose not to hide behind culture, tradition, and reputation. It was hard enough to finally tell my parents. I'd been stressed, holding back the tears because I had to be strong. Then my dad called my uncle and I had to retell the story.

Ultimately, *he* was calling out for help. I came into his path because I was the one who would be able to get him that help. I meet his parents on the night of his arrest and I tell his family, "He needs psychological help, but he's so smart that he'd outsmart the psychologists," and they all agree.

Luckily, I don't have to attend court and face him. They protect women in cases like this. A representative attends on my behalf and calls me to update me on the outcome. She indicates that they had to stop reading the log of messages in court because they were so vulgar. As a first-time offender, he was given community service, put on a five-year restraining order, and asked to compensate me £500.

I donated that money to a women's charity and I've been donating ever since. There's something we can all do to help other women who have experienced this type of trauma. This experience became an imprint in my life, and I've chosen to not let it define me.

Learning lessons

I was fighting my people-pleasing tendencies: those shadows that sat deep in my subconscious mind of not being good enough, not being loved, valued, or worthy of someone who would treat me like the queen I am. I didn't want to share this traumatic experience with my family and friends for fear that they will blame, shame, and judge me. What would people say if they found out? How would it impact my family's reputation? *His* family's reputation?

Introspection

For a long time, I replayed it in my mind… what could I have done differently? How could I have avoided this? Nothing. There's nothing I could have done differently. This was meant to be a part of my experience, and at first, that was the hardest thing to accept. Through this chapter in the book called *My Life*, I was able to acknowledge some of *my* childhood traumas — such as not wanting to burden others and the cultural conditioning ingrained in me by my community of fear of judgement — so that I could learn to reprogram them.

The experience taught me about the wounds I had that kept me trapped, like hyper-independence and control. These were coping mechanisms I developed as a child, which were preventing me from trusting that I could move through my fears by identifying the false beliefs instilled in me and choosing to love my Self unconditionally.

The experience taught me that I can release control and ask for help. It was a hard lesson for me to learn. The experience taught me self-compassion and an understanding of my values outside of my socio-cultural and familial expectations. It was a step that led me to re-evaluate everything I'd been programmed to believe. Learning about my Self and my needs allowed me to start loving my Self fully and wholeheartedly.

I remind my Self that it was *his* insecurities. It was *his* mental state. It was *his* inability to handle rejection. It was *his* darkness and it was *his* cry for help, but it was a part of *my* life's lesson.

Rachel Farnsworth

Wellness With Rachel
Transformational Life Changer

https://www.linkedin.com/in/rachel-claire-farnsworth-wellness-with-rachel-130667137/
https://wellnesswithrachel.co.uk/
https://linktr.ee/wellnesswithrachelfarnsworth

Rachel is a Transformational Life Changer. She works with clients to release trauma to overcome both physical and emotional health issues that are affecting their lives.

Rachel helps her clients heal often deep-seated trauma, while at the same time allowing them to increase their self-belief, self-worth, self-trust and self-love.

Rachel had a pattern of emotionally abusive relationships, it was so normal to her that she believed that's what love was. She also is now aware how much the sexual abuse she went through lowered her sense of self-worth, despite shelving the incident in her head and pretending it never happened. It was also why she had her thyroid removed, due to a growth on it, because she didn't feel it was safe to speak up when she needed to. Just one example of how suppressed emotions lead to physical conditions.

Rachel is also a best-selling co-author of The Power of Reinvention, Treasure and now writing her own book Decoding The Body's Messages – the body is the link between the subconscious and conscious minds.

For more information about Rachel's work and how to contact her: https://linktr.ee/wellnesswithrachelfarnsworth

FINDING PURPOSE FROM THE PAIN OF THE PAST

By Rachel Farnsworth

As a child, I was insecure and scared of life. I felt that everyone had a better understanding of life than I had. Later in life, I realised that even my birth story, which was recounted every birthday, had a big impact on my self-confidence. I was a caesarean section birth. I was told that I "didn't know the right way to come out." I had a deep sense that I shouldn't be alive. If I didn't know how to be born correctly, who was I to be alive on this planet?! I carried a deep sense of shame, I felt like a fraud, and it was a secret I didn't want anyone outside of our family to discover.

I was an anxious child at school. We often witnessed pupils getting the slipper on a Friday afternoon at primary school, so I lived in fear of that being me too, even though it was usually boys that received the punishment. Life generally didn't feel safe.

My mum was anxious and my dad was emotionally distant, both because of unhealed trauma within them. Neither were really happy in their marriage. There were bouts of arguments or periods of frosty silence. It was very often safer to be in my room and out of the way.

I was always looking for people to validate me and my opinions. It didn't feel safe to share who my favourite pop group was at school in case I gave a 'wrong' or unpopular opinion. I let my friends read my diaries. I didn't see anything wrong with that; I was seeking validation from them. I spent too much of my youth feeling anxious, insecure, and afraid of everything.

When I was 19 I agreed to go on a date with a guy an ex-boyfriend had suggested that I go out with. So, buying into the idea that everyone else knew what was best for me, I went along with it.

I can remember exactly what I was wearing that evening. I was looking forward to going out to a local highly recommended restaurant. I was wearing a dress with an autumn shade leaf pattern, with a mandarin collar, buttoned to the neck, belted at the waist, and mid-calf length. When I arrived at his parent's home, he told me to wait in the lounge. I sat on the edge of the sofa waiting for him. He eventually came into the room. I assume that we must have been completely alone in the house as he grabbed me in one quick movement and pushed me aggressively to the floor. He lifted my dress up and forced himself into me. I will never forget that animalistic look in his eye. His eyes looked dangerous. I felt sick. I just wanted it over. I felt powerless and hopeless and terrified. I dare not fight him; it didn't feel like a safe option. As suddenly as it began, it was all over and he pushed me out of the front door. I felt so dirty, so humiliated, lost, and deceived.

But worse was yet to come. I missed my next period. I was pregnant from being raped. The thought of having to tell someone what happened to me made me feel sick, anxious, terrified, humiliated, and very ashamed. I decided to deal with it myself and booked a doctor's appointment. However, my dad saw me leaving the surgery and my mum confronted me. Her reaction was devastating. She immediately said that I must have done something to provoke the rape. Not being believed by my own mother was an extra wound of self-loathing and humiliation. I replayed that scene over and over in my head on a loop, but I really hadn't done anything to provoke the attack. I hadn't done or said anything. I hadn't even had the voice to stop him.

I had an abortion in a private hospital. Mum said that I needed to pay for it financially and emotionally and then it wouldn't happen again, as I needed to learn the lesson. It cut deeper than any knife could. But I vowed that this experience wouldn't define me. I padlocked it in a box in my head, determined never to uncover it again. I thought I had dealt with it by locking it away. I had no clue that this was partly why

I fell for relationships that made me feel bad about myself. I carried the shame and guilt with me for decades.

I hadn't realised how much it lowered my sense of self-worth. I married the first man that asked me. I told him that I had been raped and what happened that night, and he said that he would have to rethink the proposal. I didn't blame him for feeling or saying this because I felt the same way. I felt like damaged goods and only deserved second best.

That marriage lasted 14 years. He put his business, his mother, and his sister before me and our children. I found the strength to leave him and we divorced, even though my mum kept telling me to get back into my marriage. I am sure she liked my husband more than me!

Four years later I married a childhood friend that had known me since I was born. His parents had lived next door to mine when they first got married and had stayed in touch. Their son and I were pen friends in our teens. I went to his first wedding, and he came to mine. Familiarity felt safe. He was an alcoholic, and I felt like I needed to save him. We were both co-dependent for different reasons.

During this marriage, my children decided to live with their father because they were fed up with the overbearing rules that my new husband insisted on. I was married to him for four years, and as soon as the wedding ring went on my finger his personality changed. When my children left, I felt broken. I didn't know what to do with myself. I worked in a school so that my working hours fitted around my children. The pain inside me drove me onwards because I couldn't stay feeling that same broken feeling for the rest of my life. One of my friends suggested that I find something that I wanted to do, and she suggested I would be great at psychotherapy. That didn't interest me, however, it did lead me to want to enrol in a counseling course. I never completed this course because we had to study hypnotherapy the first year, which hadn't interested me at all at the time. But the more I studied, the more I was interested in the subject.

I became an advanced hypnotherapist, still not realising the full potential this modality would give me. I was consumed by learning more every day and often watched training videos during my lunch hour at work. I was now working full-time at a local builders' merchant. One day I was watching a training about addiction, and I remember gasping in realisation because the scenes that the client regressed to was making so much sense to my own life. I realised that I needed to do some inner healing work of my own. It wasn't just confidence I needed. It was because I had been in emotionally abusive relationships that I had lost my confidence! That was such an incredible 'aha moment.'

I was also having practice sessions with fellow students from my advanced hypnotherapy training. A session I had about lack of confidence took me back to the rape when I regressed back to the root cause. I could see how not being believed had caused a double trauma. It wasn't just the rape itself that had had a major impact on me. I was able to heal that younger version of me, releasing the blame, pain, shame, guilt, and helplessness that I had felt at that time. So much so that I now feel indifferent to that time. It feels like it happened to someone else, a different lifetime, a different person.

Although I couldn't say 'no' at the moment the rape took place—and I am glad I didn't because I am sure playing 'dead' meant that it was over quicker and it protected me from the assault being worse. That look in his eyes frightened me, and as I look back at it now I can see that my self-protection instincts kicked in as a damage limitation mechanism.

'No more' to me means that we don't have to carry on feeling wounded and unhealed from sexual trauma. I have released all that old pain so that I feel empowered and free to live a life that I want to on my own terms. It is all possible to heal from and because I have been there too, I can offer that safe non-judgemental space which is a perfect space to heal in.

I left my last emotionally abusive relationship three years ago and had a few healing sessions around that time. When you heal at the root cause and release the emotions, it is not necessary to have countless sessions. I now help my clients heal emotional, and sexual abuse, addictions, and other trauma by healing at the root. My life is so different now. I have also helped my daughter heal from her autoimmune disease using advanced hypnotherapy too. She has been pain-free and symptom-free for over four years now. In fact, she was the first person I worked with after qualifying. She had been diagnosed with an autoimmune disease, juvenile idiopathic arthritis, when she was a year old. She was in the middle of a flare-up and was being told that she would have to go on stronger drugs by her doctors. Neither of us could face that, so we had a session together. To our surprise and delight, she was able to release the disease because she healed and released the suppressed emotional pain behind the presenting symptoms.

Just two years after leaving my marriage I am in a perfect-for-me relationship. He is loving, giving, spiritual, happy for me to just be myself, and content within his own skin. He feels like home. He had been widowed nearly a year when we met and has three lovely children who I adore too.

I truly believe that life is for living and not therapy. 'No' means to me that we don't have to feel like victims forever. None of that was your fault. NONE OF IT. It is our responsibility to heal from it so that the past doesn't keep bleeding into the present and future. Because I have been there too, I offer that safe space without judgement, so that you have that loving environment to release what you need to without countless sessions. Your future self will thank you for doing it. When you increase your sense of self-worth, self-belief, self-confidence, and self-trust your life changes in a wonderful way.

Frances Helena

Beautifully Diverse Fashion
Fashion Designer
Advocate for Social Issues & Mental Health
Published Model
Author

https://www.linkedin.com/in/frances-helena/
https://www.facebook.com/beautifully.diverse.fashion
https://www.instagram.com/beautifully.diverse.fashion/
https://beautifully-diverse.fenix360.net/

Frances is incredibly successful and well-travelled, and she never gives up on her ambitions. She never disappoints when she sets her mind to something. In addition to being a published international model, podcaster, and guest on numerous local and international television programs and YouTube channels, Frances is not only a travel blogger but also a community activist who has integrated her advocacy work into her fashion business. Frances is currently the first Australian fashion designer to be the featured designer for New York Runway 7 Fashion 2023.

HIDING PAIN DOES DAMAGE

By Frances Helena

Read this book from start to finish with an open mind and a clear conscience. How would you respond if you found yourself in any of these circumstances? How would you feel?

I was fortunate to have been adopted from The Philippines by an interracial couple, and I was nurtured as an only child with lovely pets. I have spent over 31 years living and travelling across the world in China, Malaysia, Fiji, Mexico, New Zealand, England, Australia, and many other places.

Travelling has been an important part of my life, and along the road I encountered the worst, but I've never let the worst stop me from pursuing my ambitions. Being raised in a mixed family taught me that good and bad individuals exist in every race, culture, religion, and gender, regardless of where you come from.

Despite the diversity of a biracial household, racism existed. One parent supported Hitler and hated Jews, while the other was a devoted Catholic who believed white people were superior to people of darker complexion. One parent had always encouraged me to "be different," and I applied that to everything I did. I was determined to change that mental mindset bias of 'being different,' even though challenges existed.

From all my experiences, I've learnt that individuals respond accordingly to the events they have been or haven't been exposed to. Now being older I realised that my family was dealing with their own intergenerational concerns or personal issues. This was the reason why neither one of my family members were there for me, and I never experienced family gatherings or even received birthday phone calls as we moved often around the world. I also understood that this was caused by family conflict resulting in one parent's side of the family not talking to us for 20 years.

The experiences I faced were caused because of the lack of emotional support and educational awareness of dating and sex. The trauma became constant starting at the age of 16 and carried on for the next eight years. I eventually was at a point where I kept wondering why these things happened to me, I worked hard on myself to 'be different' from how I grew up. Compared to kids my own age I had to grow up a lot faster because there was no one I could depend on. Later on in life, I understood these experiences not only affected me, but I was projecting what I had experienced onto people, especially the men I dated, I created some domino effect.

T. D. Jakes quotes "When you hold onto your history, you do it at the expense of your destiny". My history included the following:

- Age 16: sexually assaulted, a victim of a paedophile & sexting
- Age 17 - 19: raped, someone I was dating was previously charged with rape
- Age 20: abusive relationship
- Age 21 – 24: became promiscuous, was raped, sexting or soliciting sex for money, had a miscarriage, almost assaulted from hitch-hiking
- Age 25: raped

If I held on to all these memories, I would be sabotaging the destiny that God has planned for me. It wasn't until recently when I moved from my hometown to the big city, I began focusing on myself, and who I wanted to be. I decided to forgive people who hurt me, and moved on pursuing what I wanted in life, which wasn't easy, but I chose to do it with a smile. I never sought counseling because I felt someone would judge me or wouldn't understand what I had experienced, because some men I dated couldn't handle what I faced. I read a acronym, F.E.A.R., which stands for two choices:

1. "Forget Everything And Run," or
2. "Face Everything And Rise."

I decided to Face Everything and Rise, and believe me it was hard to do considering the people I encountered were searching for me.

The story begins back in 2006, a friend and I went to Malaysia during school vacation to see a relative to celebrate my 16th birthday, we had gone to the local theme park on weekends, and we met a couple of lifeguards, one of whom was 20 years old –typical me being very trusting towards anyone.

This man invited us for dinner, and on the car ride home I experienced something that would forever change my life. While sitting in the back of the car this guy was now kissing and touching me by lifting my shirt he bit my nipple hard, I remember it hurting. He started touching my private parts after he unzipped my pants, he put his fingers inside of me and started unzipping his pants while forcing me to lie down. We struggled for a bit and as I looked into the rear-view mirror for a desperate cry for help, the driver saw me before turning his head towards the windscreen to continue driving. It was a near miss when the car pulled up to the gate house, a lot was running through my mind, he kissed me on the cheek and drove off. When we got to the house door a parent was with someone of the opposite sex, who just come out of the front door – turns out my parent was having an affair.

When I went to pee it stung, and I saw blood on my bra and underwear which kept bleeding for the next few days, but at fifteen, I had no idea what had just happened. After a few days, this parent sensed something was off, and that was pretty much it. I went to the doctor when I returned to Australia, but we never told my other parent.

For my 16th birthday I got my hair braided as a gift, the woman who did my hair had a male relative visiting her, who happened to be 36 years old. I ended up exchanging numbers with his man, and he texted me constantly. My friend and I didn't think anything of it, but we began to meet this man at the shopping malls, where he would bring his niece. At sixteen, I never had a sex education conversation because it was regarded as a taboo in eastern culture, a taboo that was only for grown ups to know about.

This man kept in contact with me when I went back to Australia, he began to send images of himself, claiming that his penis belonged to me and that we were going to be married. Eventually, I grew tired of him and tried to stop talking to him – I can't remember exactly how as it's a blur, but he warned me that no matter where I was, he would find me, which was true because he tracked me down on Facebook fifteen years later. Both men as of today have never been charged.

I realised I had to grow up faster than my classmates, I became friends with families who had male and female role models, but it turns out their parents were also dealing with their own personal struggles – one family, a parent ended up seeing a drug addict for a new partner, another family was struggling because of their parents was in the army suffering PTS (Post Traumatic Stress). For me, one parent was never home as they worked overseas, while the other hadn't assimilated to western culture.

Over the next few years, I began to find my voice through these families, and myself living in and out of their houses trying to distance myself from my family to escape emotional abuse, which I later realised I was experiencing. In traditional Eastern culture, women and children were to be seen and not heard. I was a very quiet person who never spoke to anyone at school; instead, I just watched and observed. In eastern culture, family issues were kept private to result in not bringing 'shame' on the family or destroying the family's reputation.

The next seven years of my life I ended up dating men from various cultures and backgrounds. By 17 I was no longer a virgin, and a family member told me, "It was my fault, I was a slut and I deserved it." This happened because I had met a guy who was 18 years (in Australia, 18 is considered an adult), in a chat room called MSN or MySpace. We had met a few times at his work, and he invited me for family lunch, and while we were waiting for lunch we were lying in his room, He took my pants off saying, "It will be okay, just relax, it's nothing", and I was unable to move with his arms on either side of me. Afterwards, when he was done, I struggled to walk to the bathroom, there was blood on my underwear, and afterward, I never heard from him.

Not having any parental guidance made me struggle in everything, dating and friendships, I had to learn the hard way. From age 18 to 25 I dated all kinds of men, men who were charged with rape, men from countries where domestic violence was common, men that took advantage of my innocent by giving me money for sex, men who were into S&M (Sadomasochism) and wouldn't stop even if I said no, they would whip me with a belt and completely degraded me. By the time I was 25 I was already raped 3 times, and I was getting myself into all kinds of messy situations. I was in physical violent fights with women because they liked someone I was dating, and if I hadn't moved two seconds to the right, my face would need reconstruction.

At age 20 I dated this one guy when I started university, he was my best friend, and we had this natural ability to finish each other's sentences before they were even spoken, it ended because we wanted other things in life. I didn't know how to react to him because he was very kind to me, it was like I was waiting for him to turn into some monster and do something to me. Up until that point in my life, I had never been taught or witnessed how a man was supposed to treat a woman or how a man was supposed to love a woman. I resented one of my parents because they were still in this marriage which they had nothing to show for, and I grew resentment towards them for it.

Growing up I was always told to 'think outside the box, and to always stand out,' and that's what I did, I had set out to prove to myself that I was worthy or that I could do anything. After all these experiences I had a few titles to my name such as:

- International best-selling author
- The First Australian Fashion Designer to headline New York Fashion Week
- Winner of People's Choice Award UK
- Cover model for Nigeria's Sisco Magazine in Nigeria,
- Miss Photogenic 2019

During the next few years, I was living in and out of friends' family houses, I was trying to run away from family problems, and understand relationships, and myself. I had no other family, one parent had three kids from a previous marriage, the kids were 20 years older, and one of them passed away from cancer early this year (2022). I had never experienced family gatherings, never had an aunt, uncle, or grandparents come around for my birthday, and no phone calls from them because we moved constantly and then I found out why one parent hadn't spoken to their family in 20 years – it was the cause of the other parent who made us isolated, I often wondered how this parent felt, culturally family was everything.

I felt my life was a struggle, I felt like I had to look after two kids while figuring my life out, and figuring out who I was. When the family didn't have money they would steal from my account, which was opened by a parent at 16, even though I worked four jobs (in events, hospitality, modelling & daycare) there were always problems. One day a parent was going to be evicted due to the other being irresponsible, it turns out the other parent had said I was on drugs, and that was the reason the landlord wouldn't take money from me.

The parent and I got into a fight which made me angry and lashed out by smashing things, which resulted in the police coming to our house. I couldn't understand why they called the police, as this parent had thrown something at me years ago, which I ducked, and it shattered the glass window. The police rang my phone as I wasn't at the house, and they told me not to stay at the house. I went back to my friend's house, where I eventually moved out after the other parent threatened me, once I found out they were having an affair again.

The police in my life were nothing new to me, my life was deemed as a noise disturbance or complaint. Once they came because neighbours heard us yelling outside. I can't remember what the event was about, but I remember one parent pulling my hair to get back into the house. Another time the police showed up right at the scene, I was babysitting and one of the kids' parents came home drunk, they tried to push me into the bedroom, and they turned to look for something, I managed to quickly escape and ran down the street. Charges were dropped because we lived in a small town and cultural communities would be gossiping about it, and it was to not ruin the family reputation, ours, and theirs.

It became too much mentally and emotionally, I moved to the city and needed to start again, so I ended up at Victoria University in Wellington, New Zealand. New Zealand was my home for the next two years, even though I was told to come back to Australia because my family needed me. I was thinking to myself, needed me? For what? I had one parent who was in denial about the other parent having an affair, the other parent was just doing whatever they wanted, and left us financially with nothing. We lived in nice houses, and always had nice things, growing up we lived in five-to-six-bedroom houses with swimming pools or a built-in fishpond, we had drivers, and housekeepers, they were all like family though, they ate with us, and they came with us to places, and now we were in living in a rental house, with a broken-down car. The job one parent had was supposed to be an engineer-type job, they were getting at least sixty thousand USD as a salary, which mind-boggled me, we didn't see any of that money.

For the next three months as I began to live in New Zealand, I was living on a loaf of bread, a tub of butter and jam, and sometimes didn't eat at all. I had no job, so I kept looking for work. One time I passed out on the bathroom floor, a friend texted earlier saying to come to hers down the road and eat dinner, but I was lying on the floor, trying to get up. A few months later I found out I was pregnant and had a miscarriage while I was at the gym and getting ready for work. Now at 24 and had a miscarriage, I couldn't text anyone to come and just be there with me, I texted a family member, but was hesitant to do so because they were Catholic. The response I got was 'If you have a baby don't come home.' I was devastated lying in the hospital bed, the ambulance crew were nice and gave me a shot of morphine for the pain, my host family I moved in with came to see me, they took care of me, the lady of the house had passed away in 2020, but she was very kind to me, she even cut the rent down to help financially.

The one thing my life has taught me is that no matter where you come from or where you go in the world, there are good and bad people out there in every race, country, and religion. But you as a person, must find a way to find yourself, find a way to make yourself a better person. Remember that you survived and that you're an unstoppable force - a warrior who is unbeaten and won't back down without a fight. Don't let anyone take your strength away because you matter.

JOIN THE MOVEMENT!
#BAUW

Becoming An Unstoppable Woman With She Rises Studios

She Rises Studios was founded by Hanna Olivas and Adriana Luna Carlos, the mother-daughter duo, in mid-2020 as they saw a need to help empower women around the world. They are the podcast hosts of the *She Rises Studios Podcast* as well as Amazon best-selling authors and motivational speakers who travel the world. Hanna and Adriana are the movement creators of #BAUW - Becoming An Unstoppable Woman: The movement has been created to universally impact women of all ages, at whatever stage of life, to overcome insecurities, and adversities, and develop an unstoppable mindset. She Rises Studios educates, celebrates, and empowers women globally.

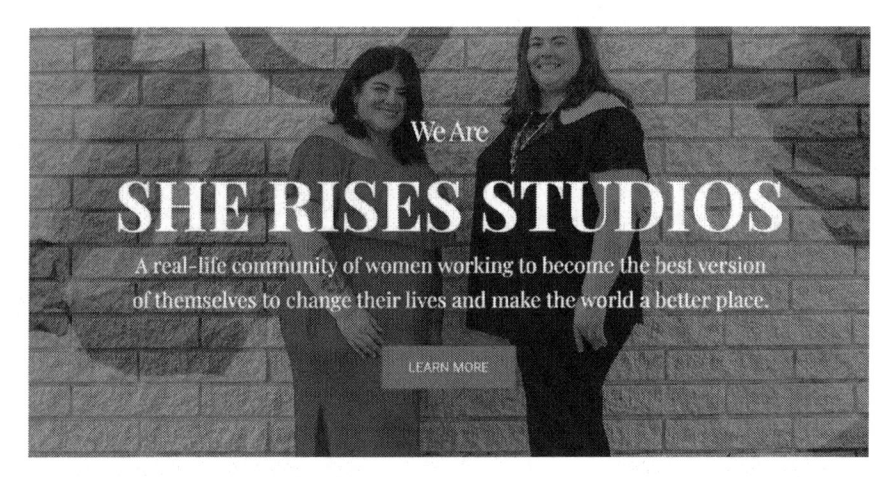

Looking to Join Us in our Next Anthology or Publish YOUR Own?

She Rises Studios Publishing offers full-service publishing, marketing, book tour, and campaign services. For more information, contact info@sherisesstudios.com

We are always looking for women who want to share their stories and expertise and feature their businesses on our podcasts, in our books, and in our magazines.

SEE WHAT WE DO

OUR PODCAST **OUR BOOKS** **OUR SERVICES**

Be featured in the Becoming An Unstoppable Woman magazine, published in 13 countries and sold in all major retailers. Get the visibility you need to LEVEL UP in your business!

Visit www.SheRisesStudios.com to see how YOU can join the #BAUW movement and help your community to achieve the UNSTOPPABLE mindset.

Have you checked out the *She Rises Studios Podcast?*

Find us on all MAJOR platforms: Spotify, IHeartRadio, Apple Podcasts, Google Podcasts, etc.

Looking to become a sponsor or build a partnership?

Email us at info@sherisesstudios.com